HIGH FLIGHT

iUniverse books may be ordered through booksellers or by contacting:

iUniverse
1663 Liberty Drive
Bloomington, IN 47403
www.iuniverse.com
1-800-Authors (1-800-288-4677)

ISBN: 978-1-5320-8764-6 (sc)
ISBN: 978-1-5320-8765-3 (e)

Library of Congress Control Number: 2019918050

Print information available on the last page.

iUniverse rev. date: 11/20/2019

This Book Belongs To:

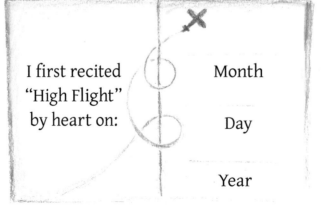

I first recited
"High Flight"
by heart on:

Month

Day

Year

HIGH FLIGHT
Words Have Wings

Christopher Lyman McDermott and Sarah Battles Franklin

Words Have Wings

Children often surprise us. I will never forget rocking my 11-month-old granddaughter and singing to her "Michael Row the Boat Ashore." As I sang each line she suddenly matched my words by humming! I was further astonished when she joined me in the final chorus of "Hallelujah, Hallelujah!" She not only sang these words but she hit the notes right with me. We sang on and it was a wonderful event in both our lives!

It taught me that we learn at any age. When I was about six years old, my parents encouraged my older brother Jack and I to recite a poem at the evening dinner table. It was a poem my parents loved to recite. The poem "High Flight" became a familiar family event. It was written by our cousin, Pilot Officer John Gillespie Magee Jr., a young WW II Spitfire pilot.

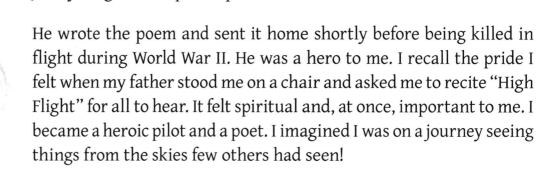

He wrote the poem and sent it home shortly before being killed in flight during World War II. He was a hero to me. I recall the pride I felt when my father stood me on a chair and asked me to recite "High Flight" for all to hear. It felt spiritual and, at once, important to me. I became a heroic pilot and a poet. I imagined I was on a journey seeing things from the skies few others had seen!

I could recite the poem long before I could read it. It has a musical quality that I hear even today when I say it out loud. The poem is called a sonnet and it is a popular form of poetry that originated in Italy. The word "sonnet" comes from the Italian *sonetto*, meaning "a little sound" or "a little song." "High Flight" carries its music in its uplifting imagery and invokes a sense of adventure.

Most children enjoy the sound of language for its own playfulness. They learn the sing-song beats of spoken poems and nursery rhymes easily. They fall in love with musical sounds long before they know what they mean.

This book tells a simple story of a boy finding a gift — and what the gift becomes! It is a wooden toy airplane made by his grandfather and wrapped in a red ribbon by his grandmother. But it is no ordinary toy. As he unfurls the ribbon, the boy and the airplane embark on an adventure page by page. Images from the lines of "High Flight" mirror and highlight these adventures. The toy plane becomes a real plane and the boy transforms into the pilot.

The remarkable illustrations by co-author and artist Sarah Battles Franklin provide colorful attraction for children following the boy's adventures of discovery in the book. Sarah is also a teacher who carefully creates each page as an active movement of entertainment for the child reader. Her amazing use of colors and storytelling images creates a supporting platform for the individual descriptive lines of the great poem.

It is our intention to provide an engaging learning experience for the lap-sitting child or a group of young students. We hope this book will serve as an important introduction to the wonderful world of spoken poetry. In all societies, significant social history has been celebrated through the oral traditions of campfire songs, tribal storytellers, and the spoken words at family dinner tables.

It has sometimes been overlooked that there are many important child development opportunities in the years zero to five, before the beginning of sight reading. Reading poems out loud with young children helps them recognize language sounds and patterns. Teaching them to memorize and perform such a poem or song or phrase is considered a milestone in their early language achievement. The more verbal skills a young child develops, the stronger is a child's sense of control. In this positive atmosphere, the child's self-esteem and confidence flourishes.

"High Flight" brings richness of color and a memorable poetic adventure with its story. I hope your child, with your help, can enjoy this book and learn the cadences and joyful words of the poem. I learned through "High Flight" that words can be wings to adventures where any of us can have "wheeled and soared and swung" and "chased the shouting wind along."

Christopher Lyman McDermott

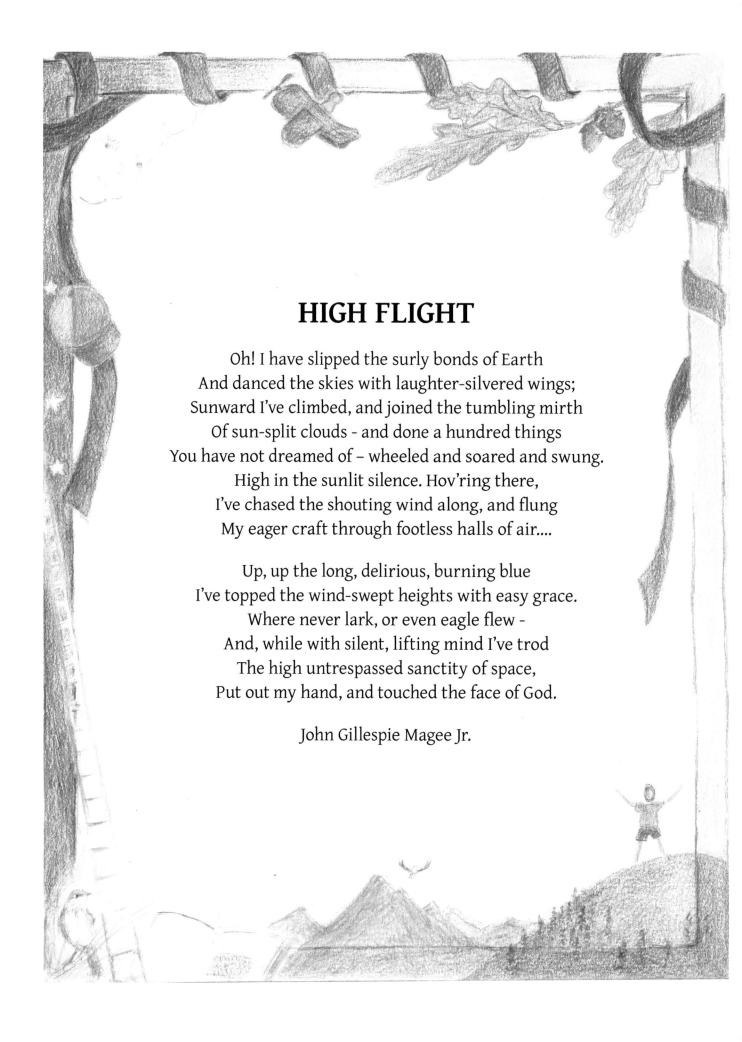

HIGH FLIGHT

Oh! I have slipped the surly bonds of Earth
And danced the skies with laughter-silvered wings;
Sunward I've climbed, and joined the tumbling mirth
Of sun-split clouds - and done a hundred things
You have not dreamed of – wheeled and soared and swung.
High in the sunlit silence. Hov'ring there,
I've chased the shouting wind along, and flung
My eager craft through footless halls of air....

Up, up the long, delirious, burning blue
I've topped the wind-swept heights with easy grace.
Where never lark, or even eagle flew -
And, while with silent, lifting mind I've trod
The high untrespassed sanctity of space,
Put out my hand, and touched the face of God.

John Gillespie Magee Jr.

High Flight

This book is dedicated to Chris's cousin, Pilot Officer John Gillespie Magee Jr., a poet and hero.

Oh!

I have slipped the surly bonds of Earth

And danced the skies on laughter-silvered wings;

Sunward
I've climbed,
and joined

the tumbling

mirth

Of sun-split clouds,

-and done a hundred things

You have not dreamed
of - wheeled and
soared and swung

High in the sunlit silence.

Hov'ring there,

I've chased the shouting

wind along, and flung

My eager craft through footless halls of air....

Up, up the long, delirious, burning blue

I've topped the wind-swept heights with easy grace.

Where never lark,

or even eagle flew -

And, while with silent,

lifting mind I've trod

The high untrespassed sanctity of space,

Put out my hand, and touched the face of

God.

Afterward

We hope that this book inspires joy of oral literature for today's children. As teachers, Chris and I have seen the gift that is received when a child memorizes a poem, when the poem begins to live and grow within the child.

"High Flight" is full of imagery that uplifts its readers, reminding us of what it is to live with courage and a pure heart. When we first met, Chris's story of this poem was of himself as a five-year-old boy, eyes shining, proudly reciting these words to his family. "This poem," Chris said, "became a family prayer." Chris went on to lead a colorful, adventurous life – always with this poem at the ready – and today can transport his listeners to unbelievable places with his spoken words.

This book is much inspired by the stories my father, Edwin Deland Battles Jr., would tell of his childhood summers spent with his grandparents and the freedom of adventure that they encouraged in him. I wish that his grandchildren, Sophia, Ada and Wynn Franklin, and Genevieve and Vivienne Schmidlen, might also know the exhilaration of climbing tall trees to find themselves deep in the blue of life.

We hope that you, and the child beside you, find hours of pleasure reading, and re-reading this story aloud until one day it tumbles off the page and into your hearts, to settle, like an acorn, in the rich soil of your being.

Sarah Battles Franklin

Acknowledgements

This book was inspired by Kathryn Frederick McDermott and Michael C. McDermott. Katie and Mike suggested I consider writing a "High Flight" illustrated children's book. Since they were raising two amazing children, Eliana and Jack, and had five extraordinary nieces and nephews – Gavin, Mickey, Jake, Blake and Brynley – such a book seemed like a good way to learn a famous poem authored by their own cousin, John Gillespie Magee Jr.

No one deserves more love and credit than my beautiful wife, Janet Sass McDermott, for her many hours of encouragement and support on this book. I wish to thank the Magee family and my dear mother, Catherine "Louise" Magee McDermott. Others who assisted us in producing this book are Taylor Cecil, public librarian, Yolo County, California, and John DeDakis, novelist and inspired writing teacher. In addition, Sarah and I would like to acknowledge the Chautauqua Institution, since it was where the journey of creating this book began.

Christopher Lyman McDermott

Printed in the United States
By Bookmasters